MW00476170

ALL-IN FIGHTING

Captain W. E. Fairbairn, in addition to having made a study of practically every known method of attack and defence, spent over thirty years in the Shanghai Municipal Police, where he was the founder and, up to 1940, in charge of their famous Riot Squads. He was their Chief Instructor in self-defence, and includes amongst his pupils royalty and several of the highest jiu-jitsu experts of Japan. He is the first foreigner living outside Japan to be awarded the Black Belt Degree by the Kodokan Jiu-Jitsu University, Tokio, and was further honoured in 1931 by being promoted to Black Belt 2nd Degree. He also studied under Tsai Ching Tung, who at one time was employed at the Imperial Palace, Peking, as instructor in Chinese 'boxing' to retainers of the late Dowager Empress.

From July 1940 the author has been Captain Instructor in Close Combat at the Special Training Centre. His methods have been approved and adopted as the standard instructions for the British Army.

In order to make the illustrations as clear and concise as possible, in many cases soldiers have been shown not wearing army packs, pouches, etc., but it should be understood that all the methods shown can be carried out with full equipment.

Captain P. N. Walbridge, Weapon Training Officer at the Special Training Centre, the author of the section in this book on the use of the rifle in close combat, is well known for his prowess with the rifle, both at slow and rapid fire. He was a member of the Army VIII Shooting Team from 1935 to 1939, while, in addition, he has been the winner of the following:

1935—Elkington Grand Aggregate. Shot at Bisley National Meeting at 900 and 1,000 yards.

1937—'The Army 100 Cup'.

1938—'The Army 100 Cup'.

1938—His Majesty the King's Medal and Championship of the Regular Army.

ALL-IN FIGHTING

by Captain W. E. Fairbairn
Late Assistant Commissioner
Shanghai Municipal Police

RIFLE SECTION
by Captain P. N. Walbridge

Diagrams by 'Hary'

The Naval & Military Press Ltd

Published by

The Naval & Military Press Ltd

Unit 5 Riverside, Brambleside
Bellbrook Industrial Estate
Uckfield, East Sussex
TN22 1QQ England

Tel: +44 (0)1825 749494

www.naval-military-press.com
www.nmarchive.com

PREFACE

by Lieut.-Colonel J. P. O'Brien Twohig

There seems little doubt that one of the causes of our failures during this war comes from the cricket (or baseball) mentality. It was the French equivalent of this which, in the case of the French nation when confronted with total war, caused it to close its eyes in horror and give up the struggle.

Unlike the war of 1914–1918 the proportion of *individual* fighting in this struggle is large, and it is not enough for front-line soldiers to be skilled in arms and determined ; *every* soldier, sailor, airman, and in many cases every man and woman, may be called on to defend their lives in sudden emergencies. This defence can only be achieved by *killing* or disabling the enemy.

To conquer our ingrained repugnance to *killing* at close quarters is essential, and no better means of doing this has been discovered than by following the training methods given in Captain Fairbairn's book.

To the civilian without a weapon or the soldier surprised without his or deprived of it, it gives the necessary confidence, determination and ruthlessness to gain victory.

It will soon be found that the principal value of the training lies not so much in the actual physical holds or breaks, but in the psychological reaction which engenders and fosters the necessary attitude of mind which refuses to admit defeat and is determined to achieve victory.

INTRODUCTION

This book is based upon earlier works issued under the titles of *Défendu*, which was written for the police forces of the Far East, and *Scientific Self-Defence*, published by D. Appleton, of New York. Every method shown in these books has stood the criticism of police from practically every country in the world, including the Far East, which is the recognized home of jiu-jitsu (judo). A more expert community for criticizing works on self-defence it would be impossible to find.

The majority of the methods shown are drastic in the extreme. In contrast to judo, they recognize no accepted rules. They are not intended to provide amusement for all-in wrestling spectators, but for use in these dangerous times as part of the national preparedness against our enemies.

The question may well be asked, 'Why should I trouble to learn this "rough-house" method of fighting?' We wish to make it clear that there is no intention of belittling boxing, wrestling, or rugby football. A knowledge of these is an asset to anyone intending to study all-in fighting, and those who already have it start off with a great advantage over those who have never taken part in these sports. No-one will dispute the effectiveness of a straight left or a right hook to the jaw or body, but unfortunately it takes months of practice to develop a good punch. Quite a number of persons, after long and intensive training, have given it up in despair. The edge of the hand blow and the chin jab, if applied as demonstrated in this manual, will quickly convince the student that in a matter of days he has developed a blow that is not only as effective as a good punch with the fist, but one which permits him to obtain a knock-out under conditions in which it would be almost impossible to punch effectively with the fist. Every method shown in this manual is practicable, and the majority of them have been successfully used in actual combat on many occasions during the past thirty years by the author or his students. They were specially selected to enable the young man of only average strength, and those past middle age, who have not led an active life, to overpower a much stronger opponent. In critical moments the trouble you have taken to master a few of them will more than repay you, and the knowledge that you can deal effectively with one or more opponents has its psychological value at all times.

Some readers may be appalled at the suggestion that it should be necessary for human beings of the twentieth century to revert to the grim brutality of the Stone Age in order to live. But it must be realized that, when dealing with an utterly ruthless enemy who has clearly expressed his intention of wiping this nation out of existence, there is no room for any scruple or compunction about the methods to be employed in preventing him. The reader is requested to imagine that he himself has been wantonly attacked by a thug who has put the heel of his hand under his nose and pushed hard. Let him be quite honest and realize what his feelings would be. His one, violent desire would be to do the thug the utmost damage—regardless of rules. In circumstances such as this he is forced back to quite primitive reactions, and it is the hope of the author that a study of this book will fit the ordinary man with the skill and the ability to deal *automatically* with such a situation.

There are very few men who would not fire back if they were attacked by a man with a gun, and they would have no regrets if their bullet found its mark. But suggest that they retaliate with a knife, or with any of the follow-up methods explained in this manual, and the majority would shrink from using such uncivilized or un-British methods. A gun is an impersonal weapon and kills cleanly and decently at a distance. Killing with the bare hands at close quarters savours too much of pure savagery for most people. They would hesitate to attempt it. But never was the catchword, 'He who hesitates is lost,' more applicable. When it is a matter of life and death, not only of the individual but indeed of the nation, squeamish scruples are out of place. The sooner we realize that fact, the sooner we shall be fitted to face the grim and ruthless realities of total warfare.

In war, your attack can have only two possible objects: either to kill your opponent or to capture him alive. You must realize that he will be fighting for his life or to prevent capture, and that it will be a very difficult matter for you to apply a 'hold', etc., without first having made him receptive by striking him either with your hand, foot, or knee, etc., thus disabling him or rendering him semi-conscious, after which you will have no difficulty in disposing of him by one of the methods shown.

We do not advocate that students should attempt to master all the methods, but that they should select about ten, and specialize in thoroughly mastering them. Although we claim that every method is practicable, it is natural that individuals should find they can master one much more quickly than another. This is mainly on account of one's height, weight, build, or, in some cases, slight deformity, all of which will have to be taken into consideration before making the final selection.

Students are warned not to consider themselves experts until they can carry out every movement *instinctively* and *automatically*. Until then they should spend at least ten minutes daily in practice with a friend. Every movement is made either with the object of putting your opponent off-balance, or to permit of your getting into position to deal an effective blow or to secure a hold. Students should first practise every movement slowly and smoothly. They should then gradually increase the speed. Pressure should be applied on the points indicated, and only when necessary. Where breaks are indicated in practice, the pressure should.be applied gradually and with smoothness—not with a jerk, which will be sure to be painful. Provided that reasonable care is taken, with reasonable consideration for the feelings of your friend, no harm other than a slightly stretched muscle will result.

It will be noted that several methods are demonstrated of breaking away from holds that have been considered unbreakable; and also that ground wrestling and holds on the ground are not shown. The reasons are as follows. The author and his students have had the advantage of trying out these holds in that very hard school of learning—practical experience, where they have not infrequently met their master. Ground wrestling is excluded because it takes years of practice to become proficient, even in dealing with one opponent. To attempt it in time of war, when one is not unlikely to be attacked by two or more opponents, cannot be recommended.

No manual of this nature would be complete without reference to the use of the rifle, and we have been very fortunate in obtaining the services of Captain P. N. Walbridge, who is one of the greatest authorities on the subject.

W.E.F.

1942.

CONTENTS

11

CONTENTS

4. THROWS

5. MISCELLANEOUS ADVICE

6. DISARMING (PISTOL)

CONTENTS

7. THE RIFLE IN CLOSE COMBAT
by Captain P. N. Walbridge

I. BLOWS

No. I. Edge of the Hand

Edge of the hand blows are delivered with the inner (i.e. little finger) edge of the hand, fingers straight and thumb extended; the actual blow being made with the edge only, about half way between the knuckle of the little finger and the wrist, as shown in Fig. 1.

1. The blow is delivered from a bent arm (never with a straight arm), using a chopping action from the elbow, with the weight of the body behind it. Students are advised to practise this blow by striking the open palm of their left hand, as in Fig. 2.

2. There are two ways in which this blow can be delivered:

    (a) **downwards**, with either hand;

    (b) **across**, with either hand; the blow always being delivered outwards, with the palm of the hand downward, never on top (Fig. 3).

The following are the points on your opponent's body that should be attacked, every blow being delivered as quickly as possible

    (a) on the sides or back of the wrist;

    (b) on the forearm, half way between the wrist and elbow;

    (c) on the biceps;

    (d) on the sides or back of the neck;

    (e) just below the 'Adam's apple';

    (f) on the kidney or base of the spine.

Note.—In the event of your opponent having caught hold of you, strike his wrist or forearm; a fracture will most likely result. This would be almost impossible with a blow from a clenched fist.

14

BLOWS

No. I. Edge of the Hand

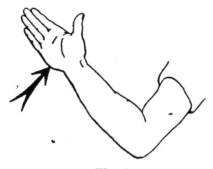

Fig. 1

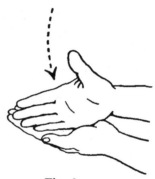

Fig. 2

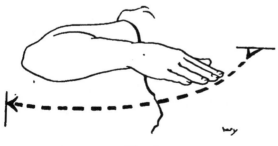

Fig. 3

No. 2. Chin Jab

The chin jab is delivered with the heel of the hand, full force and with the weight of the body behind it, fingers spread so as to reach the eyes, as in Fig. 4: the point aimed at is your opponent's chin (Fig. 5).

1. The blow is delivered upwards from a bent arm and only when close to your opponent. The distance the blow will have to travel will depend on the height of your opponent, but it will seldom exceed six inches.

2. The hand must never be drawn back, 'signalling' the intention of striking. From start to finish, every movement must be made as quickly as possible.

3. It should be noted that an attack or attempt to attack with the knee at your opponent's testicles will always bring his chin forward and down.

Note.—Students should practise this blow as follows: hold your left hand at the height of your own chin, palm downwards; jab up quickly with your right, striking your left hand as in Fig. 6.

No. 2. Chin Jab

Fig. 4

Fig. 5

Fig. 6

No. 3. Boot (Side Kick)

With a few exceptions, the kick with the boot should be made sideways. It will be noted that in this method you are able to put more force behind your blow and can, if necessary, reach farther.

1. Turn sideways to your opponent, taking the weight of your body on your left foot. Bending your left leg slightly from your knee, raise your right foot two to four inches off the ground, as in Fig. 7. Shoot your right foot outwards to your right, aiming to strike your opponent's leg just below the knee-cap.

2. Follow the blow through, scraping your opponent's shin with the edge of the boot from the knee to the instep, finishing up with all your weight on your right foot, and smash the small bones of the foot. If necessary, follow up with a chin jab with your left hand (Fig. 8).

Note.—Where the kick is to be made with the left foot, reverse the above.

No. 3. Boot (Side Kick)

Fig. 7

Fig. 8

No. 3(a). Boot Defence

Your opponent has seized you around the waist from in front, pinning your arms to your sides.

1. Having taken your weight on one foot, raise the other and scrape your opponent's shin bone downwards from about half-way from the knee, finishing up with a smashing blow on his foot (Fig. 9).

2. An alternative method to Fig. 9, permitting you to use the inner edge of the boot, should be applied as in Fig. 10.

Note A.—The question of when you should use the outside or inside of your boot will depend upon how the weight of your body is distributed at the time. Provided that you are equally balanced on both feet, you can use either; otherwise, use the opposite one to that on which you have your weight.

Note B.—If seized from behind, stamp on your opponent's foot with the heel of either boot, turning quickly, and follow up with a chin jab with either hand.

No. 3(a). Boot Defence

Fig. 9

Fig. 10

B

No. 3(b). Boot. ' Bronco Kick '

It is not advisable to attempt to kick your opponent with the toe of your boot when he is lying on the ground, unless you have hold of an arm or clothing, etc. Method recommended:

1. Take a flying jump at him, drawing your feet up by bending your knees, at the same time keeping your feet close together (Fig. 11).

2. When your feet are approximately eight inches above your opponent's body, shoot your legs out straight, driving both of your boots into his body, and smash him.

Note.—It is almost impossible for your opponent to parry a kick made in this manner, and in addition it immediately puts him on the defensive, leaving him only one alternative of rolling away from you in an attempt to escape. Further, it should be noted that although he may attempt to protect his body with his arms, he cannot prevent you from killing him. The reason for this is that the sharp edges of the iron heel-plates of your boots, which cover a surface of much less than half an inch, are driven into your opponent's body by the combined strength of your legs, each delivering a blow of approximately 75 lb. = 150 lb., plus the weight of your body, say = 150 lb.: Total 300 lb.

Now try to visualize a peg of approximately half an inch being struck with a 300-lb. force and how far it would be driven into a man's body; or better still practise the kick on a dummy figure or on the grass as in Fig. 12.

No. 3(b). Boot. 'Bronco Kick'

Fig. 11

Fig. 12

No. 4. Knee

It will be noted that this blow can only be delivered when you are very close to your opponent.

1. Taking the weight of your body on one leg, bend the knee of the other by drawing your heel slightly backwards, and drive your knee quickly upwards into your opponent's fork, as in Fig. 13.

Note.—In addition to being a method of attack and defence, it is frequently used for the purpose of bringing your opponent in a more favourable position for applying the chin jab (Fig. 14).

No. 4. Knee

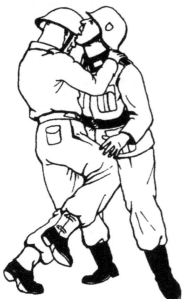

Fig. 13

Fig. 14

2. RELEASES

No. 5. Against a Wrist Hold

1. You are seized by the right wrist as in Fig. 15. Bend your wrist and arm towards your body, twisting your wrist outwards against his thumb (Fig. 16).

Note A.—The above must be one continuous motion, with speed.

Note B.—If your left wrist is seized, your opponent using his right hand, bend your wrist and arm as above and twist your wrist against his thumb. If necessary, 'follow up' with a chin jab or edge of the hand blow to the neck.

No. 5. Against a Wrist Hold

Fig. 15

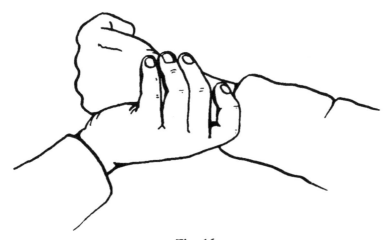

Fig. 16

No. 5(a). Against a Wrist Hold with Two Hands

1. You are seized by the left wrist, by two hands, as in Fig. 17, your opponent's thumbs being on top. Reach over and catch hold of your left hand with your right. Pull your left hand sharply towards your body, against his thumbs (Fig. 18).

Note A.—The pressure, which is slightly upwards and downwards, will force him to release his hold immediately.

Note B.—'Follow up' with chin jab, edge of the hand, or knee kick to the fork.

Should your opponent seize you as in Fig. 19 (his thumb underneath), pass your right hand under and catch hold of your left hand as in Fig. 20. Pull down sharply towards you.

No. 5(a). Against a Wrist Hold with Two Hands

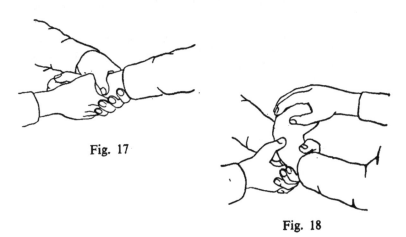

Fig. 17

Fig. 18

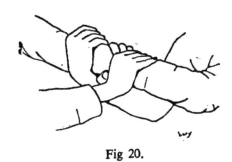

Fig. 19

Fig 20.

No. 6. Strangle (One Hand)

You are seized by the throat as in Fig. 21 and forced back against a wall.

1. With a smashing blow of your right hand, strike your opponent's right wrist towards your left-hand side. Follow up with a knee kick to his testicles (Fig. 22).

No. 6. Strangle (One Hand)

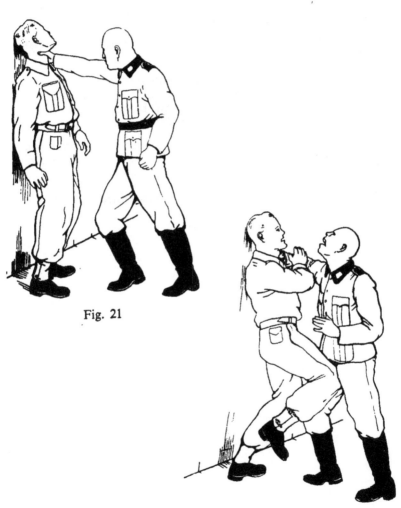

Fig. 21

Fig. 22

No. 6(a). Strangle (Two Hands)

You are seized by the throat as in Fig. 23.

1. Seize your opponent's right elbow with your left hand from underneath, your thumb to the right.

2. Reach over his arms and seize his right wrist with your right hand (Fig. 24).

3. Apply pressure on his left arm with your right, at the same time with a circular upward motion of your left hand, force his elbow towards your right side. This will break his hold of your throat and put him off balance (Fig. 25).

4. Keeping a firm grip with both hands, turn rapidly towards your right-hand side by bringing your right leg to your right rear. Follow up with edge of hand blow on his elbow (Fig. 26).

Note.—All the above movements must be continuous.

No. 6(a). Strangle (Two Hands)

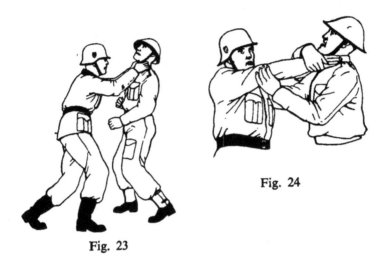

Fig. 23

Fig. 24

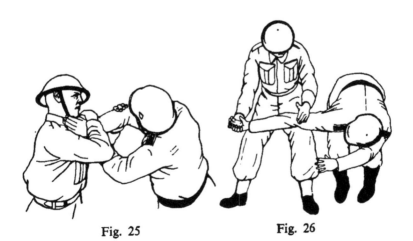

Fig. 25   Fig. 26

No. 7. Bear Hug (Front, over the Arms)

You are gripped around the waist (Fig. 27).
1. Knee him in the testicles.
2. With the outer or inner edge of either boot, scrape his shin bone from about half way from the knee and follow through by stamping on his instep.
3. Smash him in the face with your tin hat.
4. Seize his testicles with either hand.

No. 7. Bear Hug (Front, over the Arms)

Fig. 27

No. 7(a). Bear Hug (Front, over the Arms)

(An alternative method to No. 7.)
You are gripped around the waist, Fig. 27.

1. If possible, bite his ear. Even although not successful, this will cause him to bend forward and into a position from which you can seize his testicles with your right hand (Fig. 28).

2. Reach over his arm with your left forearm (Fig. 29).

3. Apply pressure on his right arm with your left (causing him to break his hold) and force his head downwards. Smash him in the face with your right knee (Fig. 30).
If necessary, follow up with edge of hand blow on back of his neck.

Note.—Should your opponent anticipate your intention when you are in the position shown in Fig. 29 and resist the pressure of your left arm (para. 3), go after his eyes with your left hand as in Fig. 30A, and follow up with a knee to the testicles.

No. 7(a). Bear Hug (Front, over the Arms)

Fig. 28

Fig. 29

Fig. 30

Fig. 30A

c

No. 8. Bear Hug (Front, Arms Free)

You are gripped around the waist (Fig. 31).

1. Place your left hand in the small of his back and apply a chin jab as in Fig. 32.

If necessary, knee him in the testicles.

No. 9. Bear Hug (Back, over the Arms)

You are gripped around the waist (Fig. 33).

1. Smash him in the face with your tin hat.

2. Stamp on his feet with either foot.

3. Seize him by the testicles with your right or left hand.

No. 8. Bear Hug (Front, Arms Free)

No. 9. Bear Hug (Back, over the Arms)

Fig. 31

Fig. 32

Fig. 33

No. 9(a). Bear Hug (Back, over the Arms)

(An alternative method to No. 9.)
You are gripped around the waist (Fig. 33).

1. Seize his testicles with your left hand (causing him to break his hold).

2. Pass your right arm over his right, as in Fig. 34.

3. Slip out from under his arm by turning to your left and stepping backwards with your right foot, seizing his right wrist with both hands and jerking it downwards. Finish up by kicking him in the face, as in Fig. 35.

No. 10. Bear Hug (Back, Arms Free)

You are gripped around the waist as in Fig. 36.

1. Smash him in the face with your tin hat.

2. Stamp on his feet with either foot.

3. Seize his little finger with your right hand, bend it backwards, and walk out of the hold, as in Fig. 37.

No. 9(a). Bear Hug (Back, over the Arms)

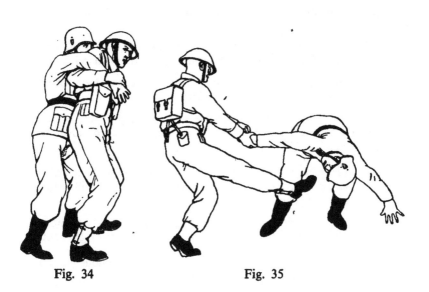

Fig. 34   Fig. 35

No. 10. Bear Hug (Back, Arms Free)

Fig. 36   Fig. 37

No. II. Hair Hold (from Behind)

You are seized by the hair from behind and pulled back, as in Fig. 38.

1. Seize (with both your hands) your opponent's right wrist and arm with a very firm grip, making him keep the hold shown in Fig. 39.

2. Turn to your left (inwards, towards your opponent) by pivoting on your left foot. This will twist his arm.

3. Step backwards as far as possible with your right foot, jerking his hand off your head in a downward and backward direction between your legs (Fig. 40).

Note.—It is quite possible that this will tear quite a bit of your hair out by the roots, but it is very unlikely that you will notice it at the time.

4. Keep a firm grip on his wrist and arm, and follow up with a smashing kick to your opponent's face with the toe of your right boot.

Note A.—All the above movements must be one continuous motion and must be carried out with speed.

Note B.—When in the position shown in Fig. 40, you can increase the force of your kick to the face by pulling your opponent's arm slightly upwards and towards you. This movement also enables you to get back on balance.

No. 11. Hair Hold (from Behind)

Fig. 38   Fig. 39

Fig. 40

3. HOLDS

No. 12. Thumb Hold

This is the most effective hold known, and very little exertion on your part (three to four pounds' pressure) is required to make even the most powerful prisoner obey you. It is possible also for you to conduct him, even if resisting, as far as he is able to walk. You have such complete control of him that you can, if necessary, use him as cover against attack from others.

The movements you have to make to secure this hold are very complicated, which is mainly the reason why it is almost unknown outside of the Far East. But the advantage one gains in knowing that one can| effectively apply this hold more than repays for the time that must be spent in mastering it.

Students should first concentrate on making every move slowly, gradually speeding up, until all movements become one continuous motion. When they have thoroughly mastered it, as demonstrated, they should then learn to obtain it from any position in which they have secured their opponent.

Students must also understand that the hold is not a method of attack, but simply a 'mastering hold', which is only applied after they have partially disabled or brought their opponent to a submissive frame of mind by one of the 'follow up' methods (Blows).

Should your opponent not be wearing a tin hat or similar protection which covers his ears, the following will be found to be a very simple method of making him submissive:

Cup your hands and strike your opponent simultaneously over both ears, as in Fig. 41. This will probably burst one or both ear drums and at least give him a mild form of concussion. It can be applied from the front or from behind.

No. 12. Thumb Hold

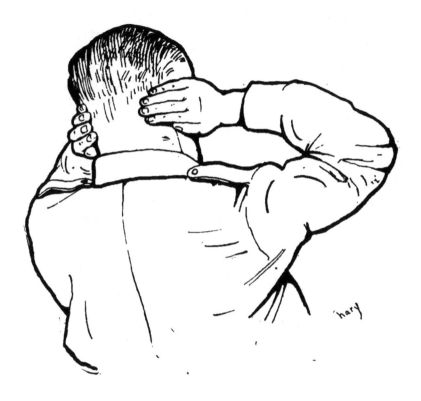

Fig. 41

No. 12. Thumb Hold (*contd.*)

Stand facing your opponent and slightly to his left.

1. Insert your right thumb between the thumb and forefinger of his left hand, your fingers under the palm of his hand, your thumb to the right (Fig. 42).

2. Seize his left elbow with your left hand, knuckles to the right, and thumb outside and close to your own forefingers (Fig. 43).

3. Step in towards your opponent; at the same time, turn your body so that you are facing in the same direction, simultaneously forcing his left forearm up across his chest and towards his left shoulder by pulling his elbow with your left hand over your right forearm and forcing upwards with your right hand (Fig. 44).

It will be noted that you have released the hold with your left hand, which was done immediately his elbow was pulled over your right forearm. Also that your opponent's left elbow is held very close to your body.

4. Keeping a firm grip on the upper part of his left arm with your right arm, immediately seize the fingers of his left hand with your right. This will prevent him from trying to seize one of the fingers of your right hand and also give you an extra leverage for applying pressure as follows:

Press down on the back of his hand towards your left-hand side with your right hand. Should your opponent be a very powerful man and try to resist, a little extra pressure applied by pulling his fingers downwards towards your left-hand side with your left hand will be sufficient to bring him up on his toes and convince him that he has met his master (Fig. 45).

No. 12. Thumb Hold (*contd.*)

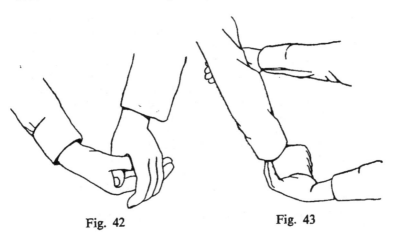

Fig. 42 Fig. 43

Fig. 44

Fig. 45

No. 13. Sentry Hold

The success or otherwise of any attempt to carry out this method of attack on a sentry will, apart from the fact that you have thoroughly mastered every movement, depend entirely on every possible condition having been taken into account. It would, to say the least, be very inadvisable to take it for granted that the sentry would be standing in a certain manner or that he would be wearing his equipment (gas mask, pouches, or rifle, etc.) in the orthodox manner.

It is taken for granted that the attack will be applied from behind; the stalk or approach to the sentry will be during the hours of dark or semi-dark; the sentry has been under observation for a sufficient length of time to permit of his habits (length of his post, position of his rifle, if carried, and his normal halting or resting position) being known; and that the man selected for the attack is an *expert at stalking*.

Now let us assume that conditions are somewhat on the following lines:

1. Rifle slung or carried on the right shoulder.

2. Wearing a steel helmet covering the back of the neck and the ears.

3. Wearing a respirator on the small of his back, projecting as much as six inches (See Fig. 46).

4. There are other sentries within shouting distance.

It will be admitted that these conditions are not too favourable for the attacker, but are what might have to be met, and students are advised to carry out their training under conditions as near as possible to those they will have to contend with in actual war.

Note.—The stalker should not be handicapped with any equipment, other than a knife or a pistol. He should wear rubber or cloth shoes, socks pulled well up over the trousers, cap-comforter, well pulled down with the collar of his blouse turned up and his hands and face camouflaged (See Fig. 47, page 51).

No. 13. Sentry Hold

Fig. 46

No. 13. Sentry Hold (*contd.*)

1. Having approached the sentry from behind to within three to four feet, take up position shown in Fig. 47. This will permit you to make a lightning-like attack by springing on him.

2. With the fingers and thumb of your left hand fully extended, *strike* him across the throat with the inner edge of your left forearm (i.e. with the forearm bone), and simultaneously *punch* him with your clenched right hand in the small of his back or on his respirator case (Fig. 48).

The effect of these blows, if applied as above, will be that you have rendered your opponent unconscious or semi-conscious. Further, it should be noticed that the blow on the throat will cause your opponent to draw his breath, making it impossible for him to shout and give the alarm.

3. The blows should be immediately followed with a very fast movement of your right hand from the small of his back, over his right shoulder, clapping it over his mouth and nose (Fig. 49). This will prevent him from breathing or making a noise in the event of the blow on the throat not having been effectively applied.

It is not unlikely that the blows on the throat and in the small of the back may cause him to drop his rifle or knock his helmet off his head. Should this happen, no attempt should be made to prevent them falling on the ground. Just simply keep still for a matter of ten seconds, after which it is unlikely that anyone having heard the noise will come to investigate. Retaining your hold around the neck with your left arm, drag him away backwards.

Note.—To enable students to form some idea of how effective this method is when applied as above, and so that they will also have confidence that it can be successfully used by a man of normal strength, we advise them to have it applied on themselves by a friend, care being taken that no more than one-twentieth of the normal force is used.

No. 13. Sentry Hold (*contd.*)

Fig. 47   Fig. 48

Fig. 49

No. 14. Japanese Strangle

1. Approach your opponent from behind.

2. Place your left arm round his neck, with your forearm bone bearing on his Adam's apple.

3. Place the back of your right arm (above the elbow) on his right shoulder and clasp your right biceps with your left hand.

4. Place your right hand on the back of his head.

5. Pull him backwards with your left forearm and press his head forward with your right hand, and strangle him (Fig. 50).

Note.—Should your opponent attempt to seize you by the testicles:

(*a*) Keep your grip with both arms, straightening out the fingers and thumbs of both hands. With the edge of your left hand in the bend of your right arm, place the edge of your right hand just below the base of the skull.

(*b*) Step back quickly, at the same time jolting his head forward with the edge of your right hand, and dislocate his neck (Fig. 51).

(*c*) In the event of your opponent being a taller man than yourself, making it difficult for you to reach his right shoulder with your right arm, as in Fig. 50, bend him backwards by applying pressure on his neck with your left arm. If necessary, punch him in the small of the back, as shown in Fig. 48, page 51, Sentry Hold, and bring him down to your own height.

No. 14. Japanese Strangle

Fig. 50

Fig. 51

D

No. 14(a). Japanese Strangle Applied from in Front

1. Stand facing your opponent.

2. Seize his right shoulder with your left hand and his left shoulder with your right hand.

3. Simultaneously push with your left hand (retaining the hold) and pull towards you with your right hand, turning your opponent completely round (Fig. 52). It should be noted that your left arm will be in a position around his neck and most likely you will have caused your opponent to have crossed his legs, making it almost impossible for him to defend himself.

4. Place the back of your right arm (above the elbow) on his right shoulder and clasp your right biceps with your left hand.

5. Grasp the back of his head with your right hand, and apply pressure by pulling him backwards with your left forearm and pressing his head forward with your right arm (Fig. 50).

Note.—Although the final position and the method of applying pressure are identical with that shown in No. 14 on the previous page, there is a difference in the amount of pressure necessary to strangle your opponent. If his legs are crossed (and they nearly always will be, when he is suddenly twisted round in this manner), approximately only half the amount of pressure is required.

No. 14(a). Japanese Strangle Applied from in Front

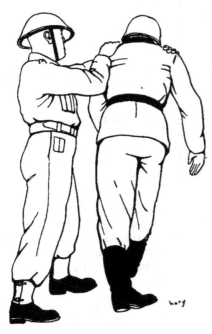

Fig. 52

Fig 50

No. 15. Handcuff Hold

1. You are facing your opponent. Make a dive at his right wrist, seizing it with both hands, right above left, jerking it violently downwards, as in Fig. 53. This will produce a considerable shock, amounting almost to a knockout blow on the left side of his head.

2. Swing his arm up to the height of your shoulder, at the same time twisting his arm towards you so as to force him off-balance on to his left leg (Fig. 54).

3. Keeping his arm the height of his shoulder, pass quickly underneath by taking a pace forward with your right foot. (It may be necessary for you to reduce your height to permit of your doing this; do so by bending your legs at the knees). Turn inwards towards your opponent, jerking his arm downwards, as in Fig. 55.

4. Step to his back with your left foot, and with a circular upward motion, force his wrist well up his back. Retain the grip with your left hand and seize his right elbow with your right hand, forcing it well up his back. Then slide your left hand around his wrist, bringing your thumb inside and finger over the back of the hand, and bend his wrist. Apply pressure with both hands until your opponent's right shoulder points to the ground (Fig. 56).

Note A.—This is a very useful hold for marching your prisoner a short distance only. A change to No. 12 Thumb Hold, Fig. 45, page 47, is recommended.

Note B.—A method of tying up your prisoner is shown on page 86, method A.

No. 15. Handcuff Hold

Fig. 53

Fig. 54

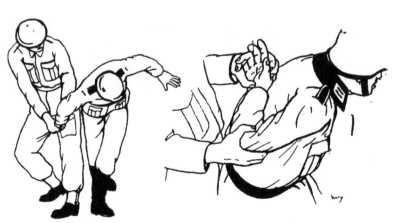

Fig. 55

Fig. 56

No. 16. Bent Arm Hold

Note.—Students are strongly recommended to specialize in mastering this hold.

1. Your opponent has taken up a boxing stance or raised his right arm, as if about to deliver a blow.

2. Seize his right wrist with your left hand, bending his arm at the elbow, towards him (Fig. 57). Continue the pressure on his wrist until his arm is in the position shown in Fig. 58.
These movements must be continuous, and carried out as quickly as possible. It will be noted that forcing your opponent's right forearm backwards places him off-balance, making it almost impossible for him to attack you with his left fist.

3. Immediately step in with your right foot, placing your right leg and hip close in to your opponent's thigh.

4. Pass your right arm under the upper part of his right arm, seizing his right wrist with your right hand above your left.

5. Keeping a firm grip with both hands, force his right elbow and arm against your chest, applying pressure by jerking his wrist towards the ground. At the same time, force the forearm bone of your right arm up and in to the back muscles of the upper part of his right arm (Fig. 59).

6. Should your opponent, when in this position, attempt to strike you with his left hand, straighten out the fingers and thumb of your right hand, placing the edge of the hand over your left wrist, and apply the pressure by a sudden jerk upwards of your right forearm, taking care to keep his elbow well in to your chest (Fig. 60).

No. 16. Bent Arm Hold

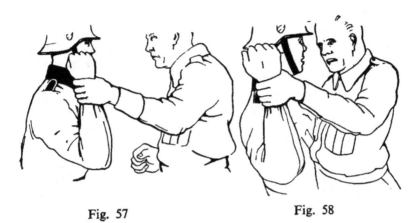

Fig. 57   Fig. 58

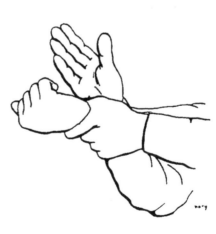

Fig. 59   Fig. 60

No. 17. Head Hold

Approach your opponent from the front.

1. Keeping the finger of your right hand straight and thumb extended, strike him on the left side of his neck with the inside of your right forearm (Fig. 61). This blow will render your opponent 'punch-drunk' or dazed.

2. Immediately after delivering the blow with the forearm, slide it around your opponent's neck, simultaneously stepping across his front with your right leg, bending him forward from the waist and catching hold of your right wrist with your left hand (Fig. 62).

3. Force your right forearm bone into the right side of his face—(anywhere between the temple and the chin will do)—by pulling on your right wrist with your left hand and forcing downwards on the left side of his face with your body.

It should be noted that the outside of your right forearm is resting on your right thigh and that the weight of your body is being forced on to your right leg by pressure from the left foot. Any attempt of your opponent to seize your testicles should immediately be countered by a slight increase of pressure. If necessary, apply an edge of hand blow—release your hold with the left hand, straighten up slightly, and apply the blow on the left side of his neck.

No. 17. Head Hold

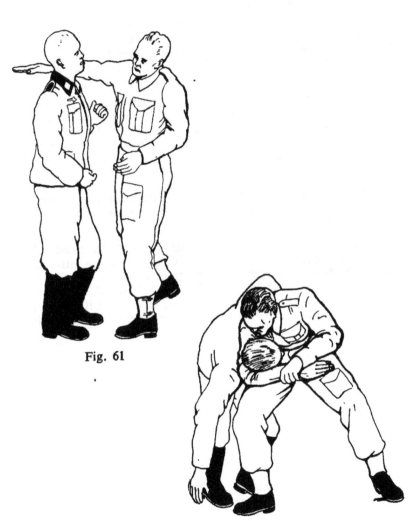

Fig. 61

Fig. 62

4. THROWS

No. 18. Hip Throw

You are facing your opponent:

1. Seize his equipment or arms slightly above the height of his elbows. Pull down with your right hand and lift up with your left hand, pulling him off-balance; simultaneously shoot your left leg as far as possible behind him, your left leg rigid and close up to his thigh. Take care that your left foot is pointing as in Fig. 63.

2. Continue the downward pull of your right hand and the upward lift of your left hand, at the same time bending forward and downwards from your waist towards your right foot. All the above movements must be one continuous motion and will throw your opponent as in Fig. 64. Follow-up with a kick on his spine, somewhere near the small of the back, with either boot.

Note.—An alternative method of applying the throw when dealing with an opponent approaching you on your left side is as follows:

3. Seize his equipment or left arm with your right hand and pull downwards, simultaneously striking him up under the chin with your left hand (chin jab) and kicking his legs from under him with a backward kick of your rigid left leg, as in Fig. 65. This will throw your opponent backwards with smashing force, after which it will be a simple matter for you to dispose of him in any manner you may wish.

No. 18. Hip Throw

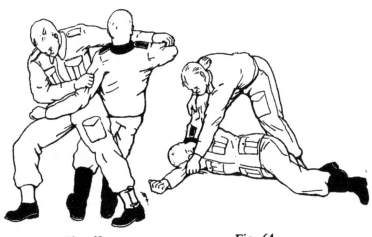

Fig. 63   Fig. 64

Fig. 65

No. 19. Wrist Throw

Owing to the unorthodox manner in which the opponent's hand is seized at the initial start of this throw, students are advised first to learn the hold as follows:

A. Your left thumb is forced into the back of your opponent's right hand, between the small bones of his first and middle finger, your fingers passing around to the palm of his hand.

B. Your right thumb is forced into the back of the hand, between the small bones of his middle and third finger, your fingers passing around to the palm of his hand.

C. Bend his hand towards him by pressure of your thumbs on the back of his hand and backward pressure on the palm and wrist with your fingers. See Fig. 66.

1. Retain your hold with your left hand, take your right away, and permit his right arm to hang naturally at his side. You will then be in the position shown in Fig. 67 (back of your left hand towards your right-hand side, your fingers around his thumb towards the palm of his hand, your thumb forced in between the small bones of his first and second fingers).

2. Bend his arm, by a circular upward motion, towards your left-hand side, turn the palm of his hand towards him; then force your thumbs into the back of his hand (Fig. 66).

3. Applying pressure on the back of his hand and the wrist (as in para. C), force his hand towards the ground on your left-hand side. This will throw him on to his right-hand side. To finish your opponent off, jerk up on his right arm, simultaneously smashing down on his lower ribs with your right boot (Fig. 68).

No. 19. Wrist Throw

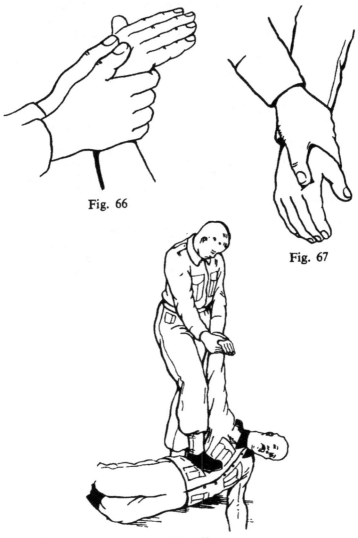

Fig. 66

Fig. 67

Fig. 68

No. 20. The Back Break

1. Approach your opponent from his left-hand side, bend your legs slightly, reach down, and seize him by passing your right arm over his chest and your left arm under his legs, just behind the knee, as in Fig. 69.

Students will be surprised, if they carry out the method as demonstrated, how easy it is for them to lift their opponent, even although he should happen to be much heavier than themselves.

2. Lift him up, mainly by straightening your legs, as in weight lifting, to approximately the height of your chest, as in Fig. 70.

3. Take a short pace forward with your right foot, bending your right leg so that the upper part (thigh) is approximately parallel to the ground. With all the strength of your arms, assisted by the forward movement of the upper part of your body, smash him down on your right knee and break his spine (Fig. 71).

Note.—Your opponent, when held as in Fig. 70, will instinctively try to save himself by clutching hold of you with one or both hands. Providing you use the weight of your body in your downward smash, he cannot prevent you from breaking his spine.

No. 20. The Back Break

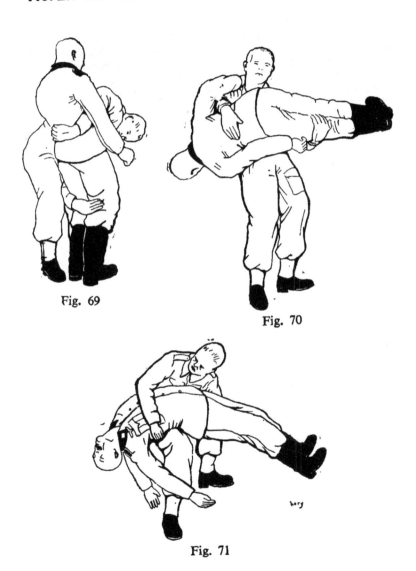

Fig. 69

Fig. 70

Fig. 71

5. MISCELLANEOUS ADVICE

No. 21. Chair and Knife

Most lion-tamers consider a small chair to be sufficient to keep a lion from attacking them. Should you be so fortunate as to have a chair handy when your opponent is attacking you with a knife, seize the chair as in Fig. 72. Rush at him, jabbing one or more of the legs of the chair into his body. The odds in favour of your overpowering your opponent are roughly three to one, and well worth taking (Fig. 73).

No. 21. Chair and Knife

Fig. 72

Fig. 73

E

No. 22. The Match-Box Attack

You are sitting down, say, in a railway carriage, or have picked up a hitch-hiker. Your opponent, who is on your left, sticks a gun in your ribs, holding it in his right hand.

1. Take a match-box and hold it as in Fig. 74, the top of the box being slightly below the finger and thumb.

2. Keeping the upper part of the right arm close to the right side of your body, with a circular upward motion of your right fist, turning your body from the hip, strike your opponent hard on the left side of his face, as near to the jaw-bone as possible (Fig. 75); parry the gun away from your body with your left forearm.

Note.—The odds of knocking your opponent unconscious by this method are at least two to one. The fact that this can be accomplished with a match-box is not well-known, and for this reason is not likely to raise your opponent's suspicion of your movements. Naturally, all movements, from the initial start of the blow, must be carried out with the quickest possible speed.

No. 22. The Match-Box Attack

Fig. 74

Fig. 75

No. 23. Smacking the Ears

This method should be applied when your opponent has no protection over his ears:

1. Cup your hands, keeping the fingers and thumb bent, and close together, as in Fig. 76.

2. Strike your opponent simultaneously over both ears, using five to ten pounds force with both hands, Fig. 77.

Note.—This will probably burst one or both ear-drums and at least give him a mild form of concussion, and make him what is known in boxing circles as punch-drunk. You will then have no difficulty in dealing with him in any way you may wish.

So that students may realize what the effect of a blow given as above is like, we recommend that they should apply it on themselves, as in Fig. 41 opposite. Care must be taken to use *only* half a pound force with each hand.

No. 23. Smacking the Ears

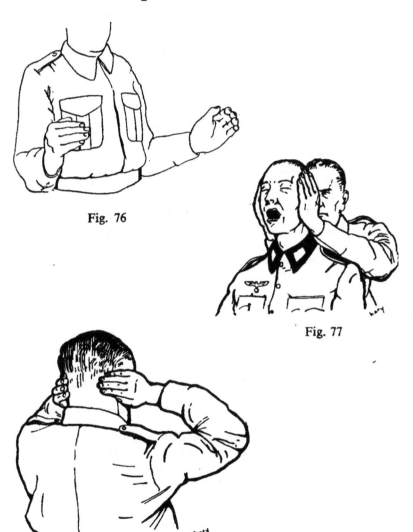

Fig. 76

Fig. 77

Fig. 41

No. 24. The Art of Getting Up from the Ground

Students will have noted that no holds or locks on the ground are demonstrated. The reason for this is:

(a) *This is war:* your object is to kill or dispose of your opponent as quickly as possible and go to the assistance of your comrades.

(b) Once on the ground, you are more vulnerable to attack. (See Method No. 3(b)—'Bronco Kick'.)

(c) It takes months of constant daily practice to master the art of falling, and personal instruction from a qualified instructor is essential.

(d) There is a vast difference between falling on mats in a gymnasium and falling on a road or rocky ground. Even a roll on to a stone or a small stump of a tree, should it press into the kidneys, would, for sure, put you out of the fight for good.

It is, therefore, obvious that you should concentrate on remaining on your feet. No attempt is made to teach you how to fall, but the following guides are given on how to get back on your feet, if you do fall or are thrown:

1. You are on the ground, as in Fig. 78.

2. Turn your body sharply towards your left-hand side, stomach to the ground, raising by the help of the right forearm and right knee to the position shown in Fig. 79.

3. Pushing on the ground with both hands, force yourself backwards into the position shown in Fig. 80, and then stand up.

Note.—All the above movements must be one continuous roll or twist of the body.

If, when in the position shown in Fig. 80, your opponent is behind you, place your right foot as near as possible to your left hand (Fig. 81), turn sharply on both feet towards your left-hand side, and you will find yourself facing your opponent.

No. 24. The Art of Getting Up from the Ground

78 Fig.

Fig. 79

Fig. 80

Fig. 81

No. 24(a). Getting Up from the Ground (Backwards)

1. You have fallen on to your back on the ground:

2. Lie flat on your back and place your right arm at an angle of 90 degrees from the body, back of your hand on the ground and your head turned towards your left shoulder (Fig. 82).

3. Raise your legs from the waist and shoot them over your right shoulder (Fig. 83).

When in this position, allow your right arm and hand to turn with your body.

4. Bend your right leg and bring it to the ground as close to your right arm as possible. Keeping your left leg straight, reach as far back with it as possible, as in Fig. 84.

5. Your left hand will be on the ground approximately opposite your right knee: Press on the ground with both hands and force yourself up to your right knee. Continue the pressure until you are on your feet (Fig. 85).

Note.—The reason for keeping your feet apart in the movement shown in para. 4 is that you will immediately be on-balance when you come up on your feet. This is a very important point to note and is very seldom taken care of by the average man. A man off-balance can be pushed down again with a few pounds' pressure of either hand. Moreover, he cannot administer an effective blow or even defend himself properly.

No. 24(a). Getting Up from the Ground (Backwards) ⁊

Fig. 82

Fig. 83

Fig. 84

Fig. 85

No. 25. Attack with a Small Stick or Cane

A man without a weapon to defend himself, especially after long exposure, is very liable to give up in despair. It is remarkable what a difference it would make in his morale if he had a small stick or cane in his hand. Now, add to this the knowledge that he could, with ease, kill any opponent with a stick and you will then see how easy it is to cultivate the offensive spirit which is so essential in present-day warfare.

1. A small stick of 18 to 24 inches in length and about 1 inch in thickness will make an ideal weapon. (If one is not available, it can be broken off a tree.)

Note.—If you are to be successful in the application of this method, it is essential you must have the element of surprise on your side, and this can best be obtained by adopting the position shown in Fig. 86.

2. Retaining your hold of the stick with your right hand, swing the other end up and catch it in your left hand about 6 inches from the end. This should be done without looking down at your hands or stick. Pay particular attention to the position of the hands (Fig. 87).

Note.—The reason for adopting this unorthodox hold of the stick should be obvious. It is not at all likely that anyone (not previously aware of this particular method of attack) would have the slightest suspicion that they were in danger of being attacked.

No. 25. Attack with a Small Stick or Cane

Fig. 86

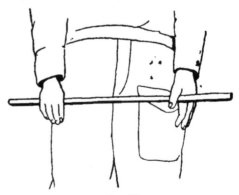

Fig. 87

No. 25. Attack with a Small Stick or Cane (*contd.*)

You are close up and facing your opponent, as in Fig. 88.

1. Strike your opponent *across* the stomach with the left end of the stick by a vicious circular motion towards your right-hand side. In delivering this blow, there are four essential points that must be carried out simultaneously:

(*a*) Your loose grip on the stick, both hands (Fig. 87), must be changed to as strong as possible.

(*b*) The movement of your left hand is towards your right-hand side.

(*c*) The movement of your right hand is inwards to the left, but much shorter than that of the left hand, owing to your right hand coming against your right side.

(*d*) The movement of your left foot is forward towards the right. This permits you to put the weight of your body behind the blow. See Fig. 89.

Note.—This blow *across* your opponent's stomach would not, if he was wearing thick clothing, put him 'out', but it will surely make him bring his chin forward, which is exactly the position you want him in:

2. Keeping the firmest possible grip of the stick with both hands, jab upwards with the end of the stick (left-hand end) and drive it into his neck and kill him (Fig. 90). The mark you are after is that soft spot about two inches back from the point of the chin.

No. 25. Attack with a Small Stick or Cane (*contd.*)

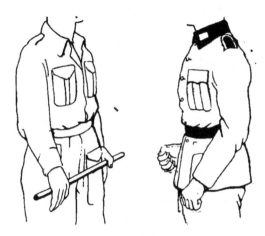

Fig. 88

Fig. 89   Fig. 90

No. 25. Attack with a Small Stick or Cane (contd.)

You have missed your opponent's chin when you attacked as in Fig. 90:

3. Smash him down the face with the end of the stick, as in Fig. 91, putting all the weight of the body behind the blow.

4. If necessary, follow-up with a smash across the left side of your opponent's face with the right-hand end of the stick, as in Fig. 92.

Note.—You have taken a step to your left front with your right foot to permit of the weight of the body being behind the blow.

5. If at any time, after the initial attack across the stomach, your opponent's head is high in the air, exposing the front part of his neck, aim to strike the Adam's apple with the centre of the stick, putting every ounce of strength behind the blow. This should kill him, or at least knock him unconscious (Fig. 93).

Note.—Methods No. 2 (the point, up under the chin) and No. 5 (the centre, into the Adam's apple) are finishing-off or killing blows, but you must first bring your opponent into the position that permits you to deal them effectively. Method No. 1 (the point across the stomach) will, on account of its unexpectedness, enable you to accomplish this, and your attack should always start with the stomach attack.

No. 25. Attack with a Small Stick or Cane (*contd.*)

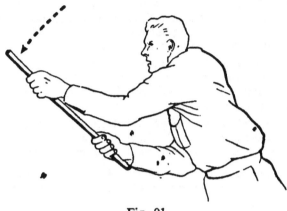

Fig. 91

Fig. 92   Fig. 93

No. 26. Various Methods of Securing a Prisoner

All raiding parties should have a small roll of adhesive tape, preferably of one or more inches in width, and a length of silk rope or cord, about a quarter of an inch in diameter and about five yards in length, amongst their equipment for gagging and securing a prisoner whom they wish to leave unguarded.

To Gag a Prisoner. Force a piece of cloth or a lump of turf into his mouth; then place two or more strips of adhesive tape, approximately four and a half inches in length, firmly over his mouth, taking care not to cover his nostrils.

Tying the Highwayman's Hitch. This knot has very appropriately been called the Highwayman's Hitch. It should be practised on a pole or on the back of a chair, until it can be done in the dark.

1. Holding the cord with a *short* end (about two feet), pass it behind the pole, with the *short* end to the left and the *long* to the right (Fig. 94).

2. Pass the *long* end, in a loop, up and over the pole and through the loop held in the left hand. Then pull down on the *short* end with the right hand (Fig. 95).

3. Pass the *short* end of the cord, in a loop, up and over the pole and through the loop held in the left hand, and form the knot shown in Fig. 96.

4. Holding the loop in the left hand, pull down on the *long* end of the cord, pass the prisoner's left hand through the loop and then pull on both *ends* of the cord (Fig. 97).

No. 26. Various Methods of Securing a Prisoner

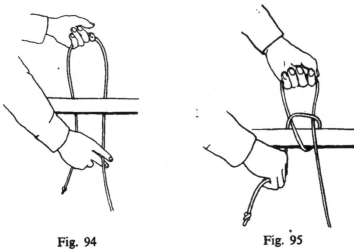

Fig. 94   Fig. 95

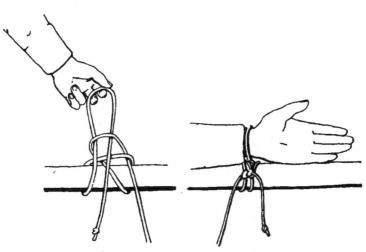

Fig. 96   Fig. 97

F

No. 26. Various Methods of Securing a Prisoner.
(contd.)

To Secure a Prisoner

A. From the Handcuff Hold.

1. Throw your prisoner to the ground on his stomach, tying his wrists together behind his back by means of the Highwayman's Hitch, as in Fig. 98, and force his arms well up his back.

2. Pass the cord around his neck; then back and around his wrists again; then bend his legs backwards and tie his legs together, as in Fig. 99.

Note.—If your prisoner keeps still, he will not hurt himself, but should he attempt to struggle, he will most likely strangle himself.

B. 'Grape Vine'. On a tree, post, or lamp-post of about seven inches in diameter:

1. Make your prisoner climb on the tree, etc., as in Fig. 100.

2. Place his right leg around the front of the tree, with the foot to the left. Place the left leg over his right ankle, as in Fig. 101, and take his left foot back behind the tree.

3. Force your prisoner well down the pole until the weight of his body locks his left foot around the tree, as in Fig. 102.

Note.—Even though you have left your prisoner's hands free, it will, if he has been forced well down the tree, be almost impossible for him to escape. Normally, the average man placed in this position would get cramp in one or both legs within ten to fifteen minutes, when it is not at all unlikely that he would throw himself backwards. This would kill him.

Caution.—To release your prisoner, two persons are necessary, one on either side. Take hold of his legs and lift him up the tree; then unlock his legs.

No. 26. Various Methods of Securing a Prisoner
(contd.)

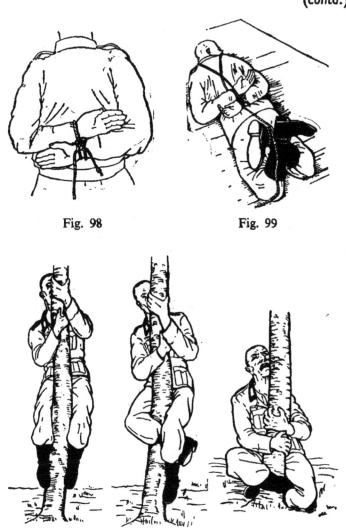

Fig. 98   Fig. 99

Fig. 100   Fig. 101   Fig. 102

No. 26. Various Methods of Securing a Prisoner

(contd.)

C. The Chair.

A chair with an open back is preferable.

1. Force your prisoner to sit on the chair, pass one of his arms through the back and the other around it, and secure his wrist with cord (Fig. 103).

2. Then tie the upper part of his arms to the chair, one on either side (Fig. 104).

3. Tie both feet to the chair—one on either side—with only the toes of his boots resting on the ground, as in Fig. 105.

Gag him, if necessary.

D. A Substitute for Handcuffs.

The following method, whereby one man can effectively control two to six prisoners, may be found very useful. A police baton, night stick, or hunting crop, preferably fitted with a cord thong, as in Fig. 106, is all that is required.

1. Cut your prisoners' trousers-belts and/or braces; then thoroughly search them for concealed weapons.

2. Make them all put their right wrists through the loop of the thong, and twist the baton until the thong cuts well into their wrists (Fig. 107). Then march them off.

No. 26. Various Methods of Securing a Prisoner
(contd.)

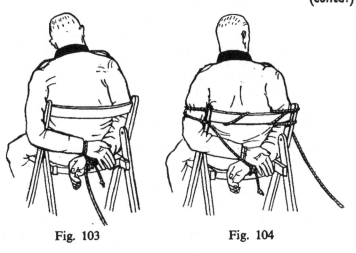

Fig. 103   Fig. 104

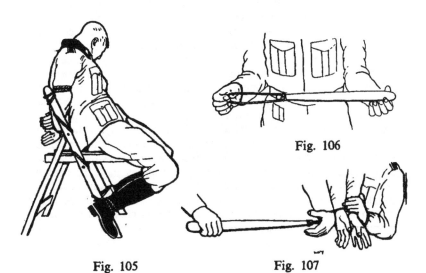

Fig. 106

Fig. 105   Fig. 107

No. 27. Break-Aways from ' Come-Along ' Grips

A number of so-called 'come-along' grips are frequently demonstrated and taught as being 100 per cent perfect, and it is claimed that it is impossible, once secured in one of them, for any man to escape. We admit that under certain circumstances it would be difficult and painful, also that it might result in a badly strained ligament. But we are well aware that any man of average build and strength can, with at least a 50 per cent chance of success, not only break away from these holds, but that he will also be in a position from which he can with ease break his opponent's limbs and if necessary kill him.

Two fairly well known holds that are so accepted are these shown on the opposite page:

Fig. 108—'Police Come-Along Grip'.
Fig. 109—'Collar and Wrist Hold'.

Students must face the fact that a man fighting for his life or to prevent capture is a vastly different person to one they may have met in competition, etc. It is an established fact that a man in fear of death will be prepared to undertake the lifting of five times the weight he would in normal times, also that he can, under such circumstances, take approximately the same amount of extra punishment.

The above is not quoted with the idea of preparing the reader to take a lot of punishment, should he attempt to break either of these holds, but simply to show him that even if he failed it would be well worth while making an attempt. One thing is certain; in the event of failing, he will not be in a much worse position than he was originally.

We rather anticipate that the reader will ask, Why is it that these holds have been so commonly accepted as being unbreakable? Our answer would be: Those of us who have made a study of the art of attack and defence well know that the average student is too inclined to demonstrate his prowess on his friends, after only a few lessons, and before he has mastered even the initial movements. This often results in broken bones, etc. Further, the counter measures used to break holds such as these are drastic in the extreme and are only shown to students after they have proved beyond doubt that they would not wilfully mis-apply them.

90

No. 27. Break-Aways from ' Come-Along ' Grips

Fig. 108

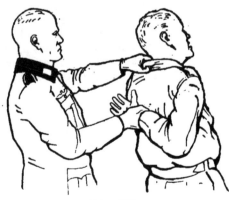

Fig. 109

No. 27. Break-Aways from ' Come-Along ' Grips

(*contd.*)

Note.—It is presumed that your opponent is not acquainted with the counter methods you intend to apply.

A. Your opponent has hold of you as in Fig. 108.

1. Exaggerate the pain you are receiving by shouting or groaning. Try to be out of step with him, which makes it easier to apply your counter. Only resist sufficiently to prevent him from being suspicious.

2. Do not be in a hurry to apply your counter. The opening will be there every time he takes the weight of his body on his left foot:
Smartly jab the outside of your right leg against the outside of his left leg, forcing his leg inwards, and break it (Fig. 110), simultaneously pulling your right arm towards you, which, in addition to increasing the force of your leg blow, also permits you to bend your arm and break his hold. If necessary, apply the edge of hand blow on the back of his neck with your left hand and kill him.

B. Your opponent has hold of you as in Fig. 109.

1. As in the previous method, wait until your opponent is off his guard and only resist slightly.

2. Turn sharply and completely around towards your left-hand side, simultaneously bending your legs at the knees and your head forward to permit of your head going under his left arm. Then straighten up your head. (These movements, in addition to twisting his arm, lock his left hand in the back of your collar.) Strike the elbow of his left arm, with a vicious upward jab, with the palm of your right hand as in Fig. 111. If necessary, follow up with a 'chin-jab' with your left hand, or knee to the testicles with either knee.

No. 27. Break-Aways from ' Come-Along ' Grips
(contd.)

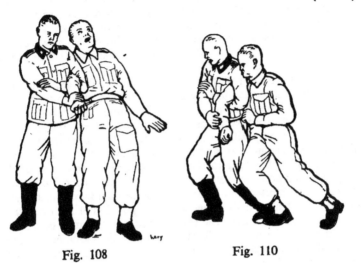

Fig. 108   Fig. 110

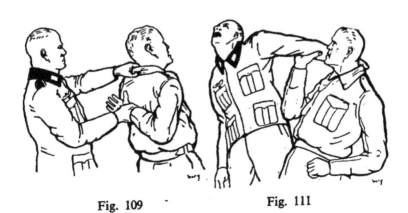

Fig. 109   Fig. 111

No. 28. Use of the Knife

The knife in close-quarter fighting is the most deadly weapon to have to contend with. It is admitted by recognized authorities that for an entirely unarmed man there is no certain defence against a knife. With this we are in entire agreement. We are also aware of the psychological effect that the sudden flashing of a knife will have on the majority of persons.

It has been proved that the British bayonet is still feared, and it is not very difficult to visualize the many occasions, such as on a night raid, house-to-house fighting, or even a boarding party, when a knife or short broad-sword would have been a far more effective weapon.

There are many positions in which the knife can be carried, but what might suit one man and lead him to think that it is the *only* position, will not, owing to the length of arm or thickness of the body, etc., suit another. This is a matter that must be decided by each individual for himself; but before making the final selection, students should note that no matter how good the position or the manner in which the knife is carried, a really quick draw cannot be accomplished unless the sheath is firmly secured to the clothing or equipment. Moreover, speed on the draw can only be acquired by constant daily practice. We, personally, favour a concealed position, using the left hand, well knowing that, in close-quarter fighting, the element of surprise is the main factor of success.

No. 28. Use of the Knife (contd.)

It is essential that your knife should have a sharp stabbing point, with good cutting edges, because an artery torn through (as against a clean cut) tends to contract and stop the bleeding. This frequently happens in an explosion. A person may have an arm or a leg blown off and still live, yet if a main artery had been cut they would quickly have lost consciousness and almost immediately have died.

Certain arteries are more vulnerable to attack than others, on account of their being nearer the surface of the skin, or not being protected by clothing or equipment. Don't bother about their names as long as you remember where they are situated.

In the accompanying diagram, the approximate positions of the arteries are given. They vary in size from the thickness of one's thumb to an ordinary pencil. Naturally, the speed at which loss of consciousness or death takes place will depend upon the size of the artery cut.

The heart or stomach, when not protected by equipment, should be attacked. The psychological effect of even a slight wound in the stomach is a point worthy of note.

No. 28. Use of the Knife (*contd.*)

EXPLANATION OF CHART

No.	Name of Artery	Size	Depth below Surface	Loss of Consciousness	Death
1.	Brachial	M	$\frac{1}{2}''$	14 secs.	$1\frac{1}{2}$ mins.
2.	Radial	S	$\frac{1}{4}''$	30	2
3.	Carotid	L	$1\frac{1}{2}''$	5	12 secs.
4.	Subclavian	L	$2\frac{1}{2}''$	2	$3\frac{1}{2}$
5.	(Heart)	—	$3\frac{1}{2}''$	I	3
6.	(Stomach)	—	$5''$	Depending on depth of cut.	

M=Medium   S=Small   L=Large   I=Instantaneous

Fig. A

The F-S Fighting Knife

No. 28. Use of the Knife (*contd.*)

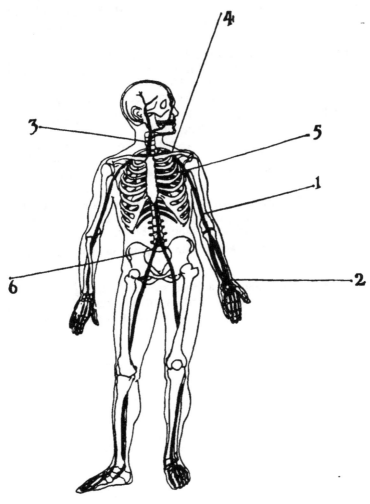

Fig. 112

No. 28. Use of the Knife (*contd.*)

Artery No. 1.	Knife in the right hand, attack opponent's left arm with a slashing cut outwards, as in Fig. 113
Artery No. 2.	Knife in the right hand, attack opponent's left wrist, cutting downwards and inwards, as in Fig. 114.
Artery No. 3.	Knife in right hand, edges parallel to ground, seize opponent around the neck from behind with your left arm, pulling his head to the left. Thrust point well in; then cut sideways. See Fig. 115.
Artery No. 4.	Hold knife as in Fig. 116; thrust point well in downwards; then cut.

Note—This is not an easy artery to cut with a knife, but, once cut, your opponent will drop. and no tourniquet or any help of man can save him.

Heart, No. 5.	Thrust well in with the point, taking care when attacking from behind not to go too high or you will strike the shoulder blade.
Stomach, No. 6.	Thrust well in with the point and cut in any direction.

Note.—(*a*) For position of arteries, see Fig. 112, page 97.

(*b*) If knife in left hand, when attacking No. 1 and 2, reverse the above and attack opponent's right arm.

No. 28. Use of the Knife (*contd.*)

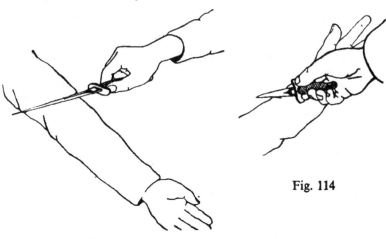

Fig. 114

Fig. 113

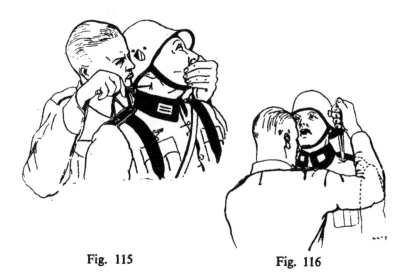

Fig. 115   Fig. 116

No. 29. The Smatchet

The psychological reaction of any man, when he first takes the smatchet in his hand, is full justification for its recommendation as a fighting weapon. He will immediately register all the essential qualities of a good soldier—confidence, determination, and aggressiveness.

Its balance, weight, and killing power, with the point, edge or pommel, combined with the extremely simple training necessary to become efficient in its use, make it the ideal personal weapon for all those not armed with a rifle and bayonet.

Carrying, Drawing, and Holding.

1. The smatchet should be carried in the scabbard on the left side of the belt, as in Fig. 117. This permits one to run, climb, sit, or lie down.

Note.—Any equipment at present carried in this position should be removed to another place.

2. Pass the right hand through the thong and draw upwards with a bent arm (Fig. 118).

3. Grip the handle as near the guard as possible, cutting edge downwards (Fig. 119).

No. 29. The Smatchet

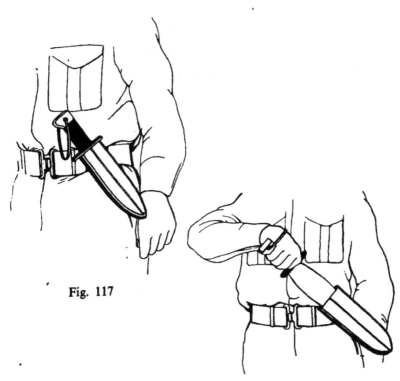

Fig. 117

Fig. 118

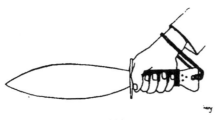

Fig. 119

G

No. 29 The Smatchet (contd).

Close-In Blows.

1. Drive well into the stomach (Fig. 120).

2. 'Sabre Cut' to right-low of neck (Fig. 121).

3. Cut to left-low of neck (Fig. 122).

4. Smash up with pommel, under chin (Fig. 123).

No. 29. The Smatchet (*contd.*)

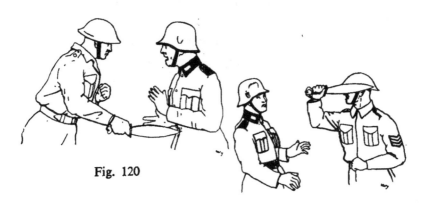

Fig. 120

Fig. 121

Fig. 122

Fig. 123

No. 29 The Smatchet (contd.)

5. Smash down with pommel into the face (Fig. 124).

Attacking Blows.

1. 'Sabre Cut' to left or right wrist (Fig. 125).

2. 'Sabre Cut' to left or right arm (Fig. 126).

No. 29. The Smatchet (*contd.*)

Fig. 124

Fig. 125

Fig. 126

6. DISARMING (PISTOL)

No. 30. Disarm, from in Front

You are held-up with a pistol and ordered to put your hands up. The fact that you have not been shot on sight clearly shows that your opponent wants to take you as a prisoner or is afraid to fire, knowing that it will raise an alarm.

Lead him to suppose, by your actions, etc., that you are scared to death, and wait until such time as he is close up to you. Providing all your movements are carried out with speed, it is possible for you to disarm him, with at least a ten to one chance of success.

1. Hold your hands and arms as in Fig. 127.

2. With a swinging downward blow of your right hand, seize your opponent's right wrist, simultaneously turning your body sideway towards the left. This will knock the pistol clear of your body (Fig. 128). Note that the thumb of your right hand is on top.

3. Seize the pistol with the left hand as in Fig. 129.

4. Keeping a firm grip with the right hand on his wrist, force the pistol backwards with your left hand, and knee him or kick him in the testicles (Fig. 130).

Note.—All the above movements must be continuous.

No. 30. Disarm, from in Front

Fig. 127　　　　　　　　Fig. 128

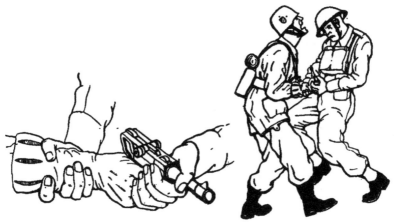

Fig. 129　　　　　　　　Fig. 130

No. 30(a). Disarm, from in Front (Alternative Method)

It will be noted that in this method the initial attack is made with the left hand instead of the right, as was demonstrated in the previous method.

1. Hold your hands and arms as in Fig. 127.

2. With a swinging downward blow of your left hand, thumb on top, seize your opponent's right wrist, simultaneously turning your body sideways, towards your right. This will knock the pistol clear of your body (Fig. 131).

3. Seize the pistol with the right hand, as in Fig. 132.

4. Keeping a firm grip with your left hand on his wrist, bend his wrist and pistol backwards; at the same time, knee him in the testicles (Fig. 133).

No. 30(a). Disarm, from in Front (Alternative Method)

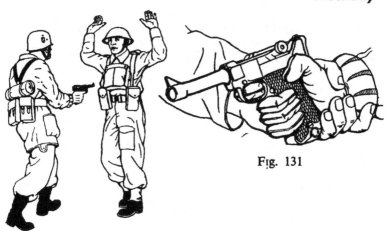

Fig. 131

Fig. 127

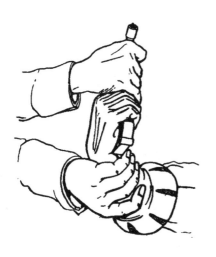

Fig. 132

Fig. 133

No. 30(b). Disarm, from Behind

1. Hold your arms as in Fig. 134.

2. Turning rapidly inwards towards your left-hand side, pass your left arm over and around your opponent's right forearm, as near the wrist as possible, bringing your left hand up your chest (Fig. 135).

Note.—It is impossible for him to shoot you or release his arm from this grip.

3. Immediately the arm is locked, knee him in the testicles with your right knee, and 'chin-jab' him with your right hand, as in Fig. 136.

Note.—In the event of the knee blow and 'chin-jab' not making him release his hold of the pistol, go after his eyes with the fingers of your right hand.

No. 30(b). Disarm, from Behind

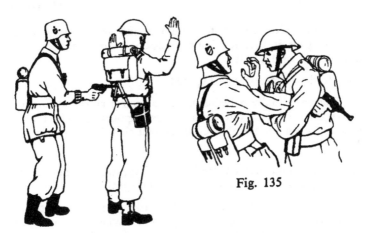

Fig. 134

Fig. 135

Fig. 136

No. 30(c). Disarm, from Behind (Alternative Method)

The difference between this method and that shown on the previous page is that the initial attack is made with your right arm instead of the left.

1. Hold your arms as in Fig. 134.

2. Turning rapidly outwards towards your right-hand side, pass your right arm over and around your opponent's right forearm, as near the wrist as possible, bringing your right hand up your chest (Fig. 137).

Note.—As in the previous method, it is impossible for him to shoot you or release his arm from this grip.

3. Immediately the arm is locked, strike your opponent across the throat, as near the Adam's apple as possible, with an edge-of-the-hand blow, with your left hand, as in Fig. 138.

Note.—Should your opponent not release his hold of the pistol, follow-up by pressing with your right leg on the outside of his right leg, as in Fig. 139, and break his leg.

No. 30(c). Disarm, from Behind (Alternative Method)

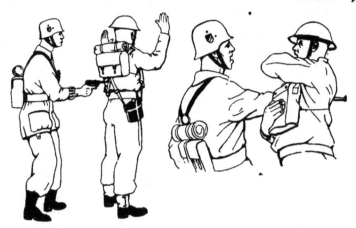

Fig. 134   Fig. 137

Fig. 138   Fig. 139

No. 30(d). Disarming a Third Party

It is not at all unlikely you might, upon coming round a corner, find one of your own men being held up, as in Fig. 140.

1. Come up on the opponent's pistol arm, seize his pistol and hand from underneath, simultaneously coming down hard with your left hand on his arm, just above the elbow joint (Fig. 141).

2. Jerk his hand upwards and backwards, and force his elbow upwards with your left hand, at the same time pivoting inwards on your left foot. Continue the pressure of your right hand in a downward direction (Fig. 142).

Note A.—This will cause him to release his hold of the pistol; if necessary, knee him in the testicles with your right knee.

Note B.—The reason why we recommend the initial upward movement of the pistol (para. 2) in preference to a downward blow is that the pistol is jerked away from the direction of your own man very quickly, and it also permits you to obtain a hold of his pistol hand, from which you can force him to release his hold of the weapon. Further, your own man can, by means of a kick to the opponent's testicles, considerably help you in disarming.

If you are inclined to think these methods are 'not cricket', remember that Hitler does not play this game.

W.E.F.

No. 30(d). Disarming a Third Party

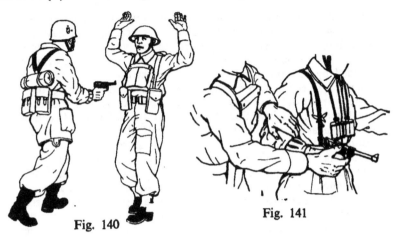

Fig. 140

Fig. 141

Fig. 142

7. THE RIFLE IN CLOSE COMBAT

by Captain P. N. Walbridge

From the work of Captain W. E. Fairbairn you will have obtained some wonderful methods of attack and defence. He will have instilled into you a real fighting spirit and a willingness for close combat. I write only of the use of the rifle and bayonet—a weapon regarded by far too many people as almost obsolete.

Many manuals have been written on the methods of firing, most of them suited only to peace-time conditions and to slow shooting. It is, therefore, the intention of these pages (in as few words and as few lessons as possible) to help to bring back the rifle to its rightful position and real use, and to enable any man to reach a standard of efficiency in handling that will surprise even the expert.

The reader will appreciate that it is necessary to explain a few points about elementary work before advancing to rapid firing.

The rifle is a far more efficient weapon than is generally recognized, and can be used with deadly effect at short ranges in the manner of a sub-machine gun, besides being the best friend at longer distances.

The use of the Short Magazine Lee Enfield (S.M.L.E.) will be assumed, but the same methods may be applied to the Pattern 14 (P. 14) or the .300 American rifle.

It must be borne in mind that the rifle must shoot 'straight'. Errors in elevation can be corrected by backsight adjustment or by aiming up or down. The rifle must never have a lateral error. Test it at a short range, either 25 or 100 yards, and if it is shooting to the left or right, the foresight must be moved. This adjustment is very easily carried out provided you remember that the foresight must be moved in the same direction as the error, i.e. if the shots are to the right, the foresight must be moved to the right; and vice versa.

Preparation of the Rifle

Remove the bolt, magazine, and magazine platform. With the aid of a pull-through and flannelette, dry-clean the barrel until all trace of oil is removed. With a stick of suitable size (Fig. 143) and a piece of flannelette, clean out the chamber. This is a most important part in preparation, as the presence of dirt or oil in the chamber will prevent the cartridge from being easily withdrawn, and cause unnecessary delay in re-loading. Remove all trace of oil and dirt from the body of the rifle and the inside of the magazine. Clean the outside, ensuring that the foresight and backsight are free from oil. Thoroughly dry-clean the bolt. Lightly oil the bolt and along the inside of the body of the rifle. Keep the face of the bolt dry. The rifle is now ready for use.

Note.—Care should be taken in the cleaning of 'browned' metal parts. Rub lightly to avoid the browning being removed.

Fig. 143

Aiming

With the S.M.L.E., aim should always be taken by having the foresight in the centre of the 'U' of the backsight and in line with the top of the shoulders (Fig. 144). With the aperture backsight, the foresight must be seen in the centre of the aperture (Fig. 145). With this type of sight, ignore the backsight and *concentrate on the foresight*. The eye will automatically tend to centre it in the aperture, which is generally so small that it permits of few errors. With both sights, aim will always be taken at the centre of the target.

Aiming

Fig. 144

Fig. 145

THE RIFLE IN CLOSE COMBAT

Aiming

To enable you to practise aiming on your own, fix your rifle in any convenient way (such as between two sandbags, or on a folded coat) and aim at a prepared target with a hole made at the point of aim (Fig. 146). You are then able to go behind the target and glance back at your sights through the small hole, thus obtaining the view from the 'bullet end'. Errors in aiming will be easy to detect. Fig. 147 shows a correct aim. Fig. 148 shows a low left aim. As a result of this error, the shot would go low and to the left. Fig. 149 shows a high right aim, and in this case the shot would go high and to the right. Constant practice in aiming is necessary to eliminate faults. Occasionally practise aiming with both eyes open, as the left eye is seldom closed in quick firing.

Aiming

Fig. 146

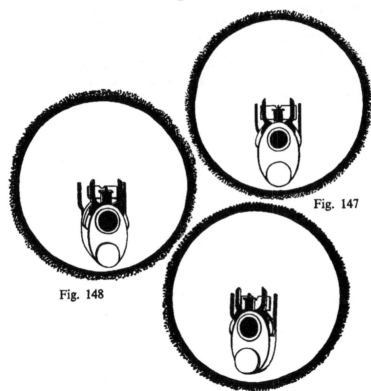

Fig. 147

Fig. 148

Fig. 149

Loading

For quick, clean loading, careful preparation of the charger is essential.

First, ensure that the ammunition and charger are clean; then place the rounds in as shown in Fig. 150, 'one up', 'one down'. Remove and replace them quickly to ensure that the charger works freely. Ninety per cent of jams that occur in loading are due to bad filling of the chargers.

To load, push forward the safety catch, pull out the cut-off (if any), place the charger in the rifle and the right hand and thumb in position, as in Fig. 151. Push the rounds into the magazine in one movement, close the breech, and apply the safety catch.

If the rifle is to remain loaded for a very long period, it is advisable to push the top round down and close the breech on an empty chamber; press the trigger and apply the safety catch. This will avoid the bolt main spring being compressed. When required for use, push forward the safety catch, open the cut-off, and open and close the breech.

Loading

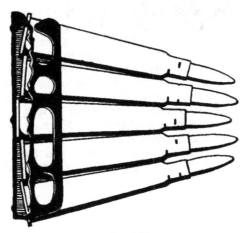

Fig. 150

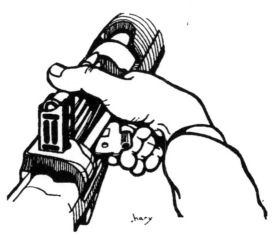

Fig. 151

THE RIFLE IN CLOSE COMBAT

Firing Positions

The basic firing position from which to teach yourself quick and clean manipulation of the rifle is the lying position. This should be adopted as shown in Fig. 152. Notice especially (1) the relative closeness of the elbows, and (2) the forward position of the rifle. Careful attention to these particular points will enable you to use the elbows as a pivot to bring the rifle to the aiming position. No other movement of the body is then necessary. The position of the legs (open or crossed) is immaterial so long as the firer is comfortable. In the aiming position (Fig. 153), hold the rifle firmly back into the shoulder with the left hand, press the cheek firmly on the butt (producing a locking effect), and hold lightly with the right hand. This allows quick and delicate handling of the trigger.

Trigger Pressing

After the rifle has been brought to the shoulder, without undue delay take the first pressure, breathing naturally until you are ready to fire. Then lightly restrain the breathing, and fire. Keep your right eye open the whole time and try to observe the strike of your shot.

Firing Positions

Fig. 152

Fig. 153

THE RIFLE IN CLOSE COMBAT

Quick Handling

Let me stress at once that, in rapid firing, each shot is fired in exactly the same manner as a slow shot. The number of rounds you are able to fire in one minute will depend on the length of time it takes you to open and close the breech. When re-loading, only the slightest movement of the right hand and wrist is necessary. Hold the knob of the bolt firmly between the thumb and forefinger; raise it, at the same time tilting the rifle slightly to the right; draw the bolt fully to the rear, and at once close the breech with a sharp forward and downward movement. All these actions should be continuous, and carried out as quickly as possible after the shot has been fired. The action of tilting the rifle will assist the opening of the breech and the ejection of the empty case. The head must be kept still throughout. To enable you to get correct bolt manipulation, practise in the following way. Tie the trigger to the rear (Fig. 154). Then, in the lying position, practise the correct movement of the right hand and wrist in opening and closing the breech. Place the right hand in its correct position and the finger on the trigger each time.

Note.—Tying back the trigger will make practice in manipulation easier, and will prevent unnecessary wear to the face of the cocking piece, and avoid weakening the bolt main spring. On the P.14 and .300 American rifle, it will also be necessary to remove the magazine platform and spring.

When you have mastered the wrist and hand movement so essential to good manipulation, remove the string and practise firing. Each day will see a great change in your ability to fire a large number of accurately aimed shots. Quick inaccurate shooting is of no use. Each shot must be fired by taking the first and second pressures correctly. Only in this way can you hope to become an expert in rapid firing. Try and keep to the suggested programme.

1st day—1 hour: manipulation, with trigger tied.
2nd day—1 hour: manipulation and slow shooting.
3rd day—1 hour: practise firing 15 accurate shots in one minute.
4th day—1 hour: increase to 20 rounds in one minute.
5th day—1 hour: increase to 25 rounds in one minute.
6th day—1 hour: increase to 30 rounds in one minute.

126

Quick Handling (*contd.*)

The above standards are set assuming you will not be able to obtain dummy cartridges. If you train to fire thirty aimed shots in one minute in this manner, you should be capable of firing twenty to twenty-five rounds of ball ammunition in one minute and maintain reasonable accuracy. Get a friend to assist you. He can correct your aims either by (1) glancing through the small hole of a prepared target as described in 'Aiming', or (2) by letting you aim at his eye, previously making sure that the rifle is unloaded. It will be observed that the above programme allows you only six hours to become an expert in rapid fire. This is not impossible. Provided reasonable efficiency has been attained in slow firing, you should now be ready to quicken up.

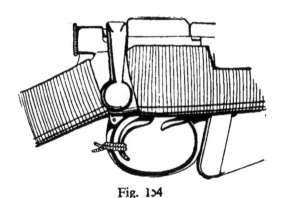

Fig. 154

Close-Quarter Fighting

In close fighting, such as in streets, clearing woods, etc., speed is essential. You will seldom be given the opportunity to adopt a comfortable firing position, but will have to fire either from the hip (Fig. 155) or from the shoulder whilst in the standing position. In firing from the hip, you must be very close to your target if you are to obtain a hit, whereas from the shoulder, firing is much quicker and accuracy is not so much sacrificed. When approaching an area where your target is likely to appear suddenly, e.g. stalking a mortar post or machine-gun nest, etc., carry the rifle as shown in Fig. 156. This will enable you instantly to bring the rifle to the shoulder and open fire. To increase your speed of firing to a rate previously imagined unattainable, you will have to press the trigger with the first or second finger while retaining your hold on the bolt (Fig. 157) and ignore the fact that the trigger has two pressures.

In this way, you should, after a few hours' practice, be able to fire five shots in four seconds. For close work or crossing a gap, you will find it invaluable to be able to fire at this speed with reasonable accuracy. I have frequently fired at a much faster rate when demonstrating this method.

Fifteen minutes' manipulation and firing daily will increase your · handling ability and speed by 100 per cent.

Close-Quarter Fighting

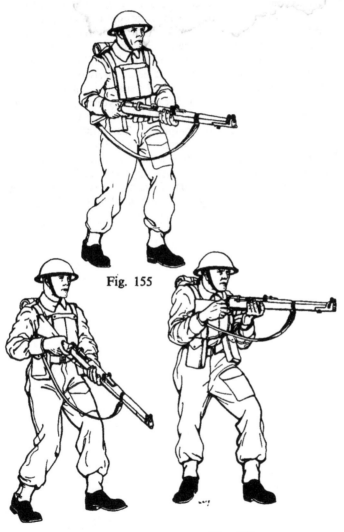

Fig. 155

Fig. 156   Fig. 157

THE RIFLE IN CLOSE COMBAT

The Bayonet

The bayonet will be used in close hand-to-hand fighting where you have no time to reload, or more probably when your magazine is empty. Otherwise you would shoot from the hip or shoulder. Except when in close formation among comrades, *keep the bayonet point low*. Carry the rifle as shown in Fig. 158. In this position there is less chance of your thrust being parried and you are able to deliver a point in any direction. To make a point, lunge forward on either foot and drive the point of the bayonet into the pit of your opponent's stomach (Fig. 159). Most of the upper part of the body will be covered by equipment. To withdraw, take a short pace to the rear as you wrench out the bayonet. You are then in a good position to deliver a second point, should this become necessary. If you are close to your opponent and unable to deliver a point, smash him on the side of his head with the butt (Fig. 160) and follow up with the bayonet or any method previously described.

The Bayonet

Fig. 158   Fig. 159

Fig. 160

Cleaning the Rifle after Use

Strip the rifle as already explained in the lesson on Preparation of the Rifle. Clean the barrel with dry flannelette until most of the fouling has been removed. By means of a funnel or a kettle with a thin spout pour either cold or hot water through the barrel. Boiling water should be used whenever possible (about two pints is sufficient). Dry-clean the barrel until all trace of fouling has been removed, and when the barrel is cool, it must be oiled. Clean and lightly oil the outside of the rifle. Special care and attention should be given to the rifle for a period of five days after firing, as during this period the barrel will 'sweat' and will be liable to turn rusty. The barrel must be dry-cleaned and again re-oiled each day. If water is not available, immediately firing has ceased the rifle-barrel must be well oiled, and the first opportunity taken to clean it as already described. When putting the rifle away after cleaning, it is advisable to stand it upside down. This will prevent the oil from the barrel entering the bolt, and avoid the possibility of a splash of oil from the cocking piece getting into the firer's eyes. If linseed oil is obtainable it should be lightly applied to the woodwork.

Note.—Care must be taken to ensure that water does not enter between the woodwork and the barrel.